Roman Numerals

Although we usually use Arabic numerals, Roman numerals are still often used on clocks, buildings, pages of books, and elsewhere.

This introduction to Roman numerals shows how the Romans developed their system of numbers and how Roman numerals are written—from the simple I to a discussion of the historic relationship between the V and X; to the more difficult subtraction idea in the IV, which early Romans wrote as IIII. Using coins, paper, cardboard, scissors, and a pencil, the young mathematician will become involved in learning the principles behind writing Roman numerals.

Byron Barton, the illustrator, has created an amusing Roman stonecutter who carefully clarifies the text.

Roman Numerals

by David A. Adler
illustrated by Byron Barton

Thomas Y. Crowell   New York

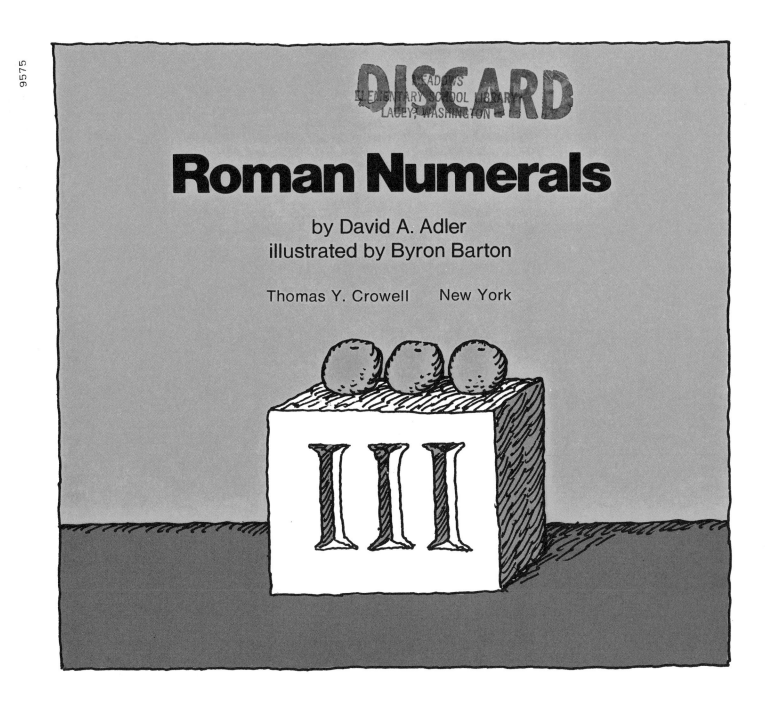

YOUNG MATH BOOKS

Edited by Dr. Max Beberman, Director of the Committee on
School Mathematics Projects, University of Illinois

BIGGER AND SMALLER
by Robert Froman

CIRCLES
by Mindel and Harry Sitomer

COMPUTERS
by Jane Jonas Srivastava

THE ELLIPSE
by Mannis Charosh

ESTIMATION
by Charles F. Linn

FRACTIONS ARE PARTS OF THINGS
by J. Richard Dennis

GRAPH GAMES
by Frédérique and Papy

LINES, SEGMENTS, POLYGONS
by Mindel and Harry Sitomer

LONG, SHORT, HIGH, LOW, THIN, WIDE
by James T. Fey

MATHEMATICAL GAMES FOR ONE OR TWO
by Mannis Charosh

ODDS AND EVENS
by Thomas C. O'Brien

PROBABILITY
by Charles F. Linn

RIGHT ANGLES: PAPER-FOLDING GEOMETRY
by Jo Phillips

RUBBER BANDS, BASEBALLS AND DOUGHNUTS:
A BOOK ABOUT TOPOLOGY
by Robert Froman

STRAIGHT LINES, PARALLEL LINES,
PERPENDICULAR LINES
by Mannis Charosh

WEIGHING & BALANCING
by Jane Jonas Srivastava

WHAT IS SYMMETRY?
by Mindel and Harry Sitomer

Edited by Dorothy Bloomfield, Mathematics Specialist,
Bank Street College of Education

LESS THAN NOTHING IS REALLY SOMETHING *by Robert Froman*

STATISTICS *by Jane Jonas Srivastava*

VENN DIAGRAMS *by Robert Froman*

Library of Congress Cataloging in Publication Data. Adler, David A. Roman numerals. SUMMARY: Explains the Roman numeral
system, which, though very old, is still in use today. 1. Roman numerals—Juv. lit. 1. Roman numerals I. Barton, Byron. II Title.
QA141.3.A34 513'.2 77-2270 ISBN 0-690-01302-7

Roman Numerals

Did you know that many years ago ♀ was a numeral? It meant 100. ∩ meant 10 and | meant 1.. Today if you write ∩∩∩|| few people will know what you mean. But in Egypt many years ago people knew that ∩∩∩|| meant 32.

There are other number systems which used

numerals that look very different from the numerals we use today.

Did you know that $<$ once meant 10 and $\vee$ once meant 1?

Today if you write $<<<<\vee\vee$ few people will know what you mean. But in Babylonia many years ago people knew that $<<<\vee\vee$ meant 32.

Roman numerals are also old and very different from the numerals we usually use today. But if you write XXXII most people will know that you have written the number 32. People know that XXXII means 32 because today people still use Roman numerals.

The numbers on some clocks are written with Roman numerals.

On the sides of some buildings the year that the building was built is written with Roman numerals.

In many books Roman numerals are used to number some pages. Roman numerals are sometimes also used to number chapters.

I is the symbol the Romans used for 1. In Roman numerals II means 2. III means 3. In the beginning the Romans wrote IIII when they meant 4.

If there were only one symbol in Roman numerals it would take a long time to write and to read large numbers. Take a pencil and paper and write the number 32 by writing the symbol I thirty-two times.

This is not an easy way to write a large number. Even after you have written it, it isn't easy to tell what number it is.

Because it would be so difficult to use the same symbol over and over, the Romans added other symbols to their system.

Hold up your hand. Put your five fingers together. If you separate your thumb from your other fingers, you can see where the Roman symbol for 5 may have come from.

What letter have you formed with your fingers? Have you formed the letter V? In Roman numerals the symbol for 5 is V.

In Roman numerals there is also a symbol for 10. Take a pencil and paper. Write the Roman symbol for 5. Now turn the paper so that it is upside down. Write the Roman symbol for 5 again so that the bottoms of the first 5 and the second 5 are touching.

What letter have you formed? Some people believe that X, the Roman symbol for 10, came from the letter formed by putting together two Roman symbols for 5. Other people who have

studied Roman numerals believe that X, the symbol for 10, came first. Then V, the top half of X, was chosen for half of 10.

In Roman numerals:
I means 1,
V means 5,
X means 10.

The Romans used addition to write numbers. In Roman numerals II means 1 + 1, or 2. VI means 5 + 1, or 6. How do you think they wrote 7? 8? 9?

X is the symbol for 10. XI means 10 + 1, or 11. How do you think we write 12 and 13 in Roman numerals?

XVI means 10 + 5 + 1, or 16.

XXII means 10 + 10 + 1 + 1, or 22.

How do you think we write 17, 18, 23, and 25 in Roman numerals?

Look back over the numbers we have written. To write a number in Roman numerals, first you must choose the proper symbols. Then the symbols must be put in the proper order.

For example, X, V, I, and I are the symbols you need to write 17. But IIVX, and XIVI do not mean 17. In Roman numerals 17 is always written XVII.

Correct

When we write Roman numerals we must put the symbols in the proper order. We show we are adding when we write the symbols with the largest value first.

Here is something that you can do. It will help you to understand how to put Roman symbols in the proper order.

You will need:

a pencil,
scissors,
and either cardboard
or paper.

Cut out three squares of cardboard (or paper) all about this size.

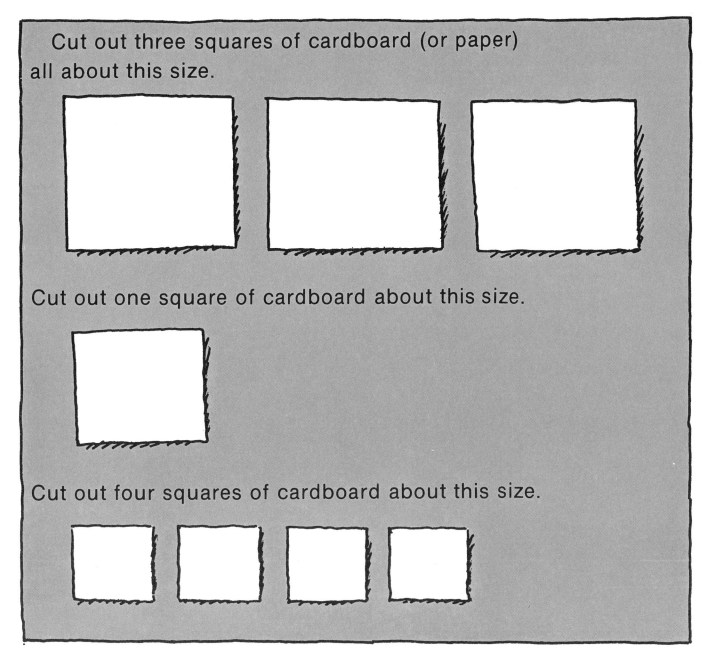

Cut out one square of cardboard about this size.

Cut out four squares of cardboard about this size.

On one side of each large square write 10. On the other side write X.

On one side of the middle-sized square write 5. On the other side write V.

On one side of each of the small squares write 1. On the other side write I.

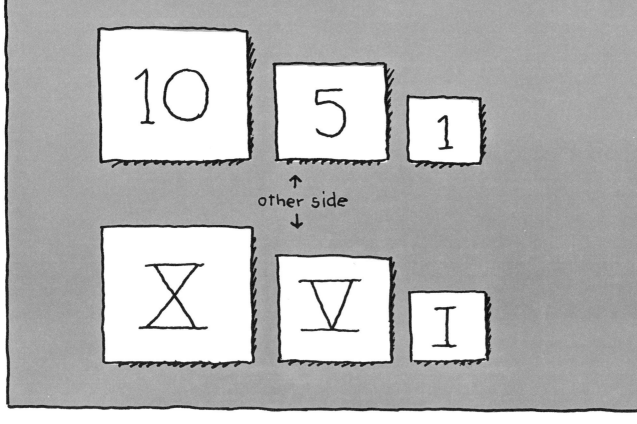

other side

Turn all the cards so that you see only 1's, 5, and 10's.

Now take enough cards so that the numbers together make 27. Turn the cards over and put them in order. Put the largest cards first, then the middle-sized card, and then the smallest cards.

When you put the cards in order you should have XXVII. In Roman numerals XXVII is 27.

Put all the cards together again and turn them so that you see only 1's, 5, and 10's.

Take the cards that together make 31. Turn the cards over and put them in order. You should have XXXI. In Roman numerals XXXI means 31.

Put all the cards together again and turn them so that you see only 1's, 5, and 10's.

Take the cards that together make 38. Turn the cards over and put them in order. You should have XXXVIII. In Roman numerals XXXVIII means 38. When we write Roman numerals we must put the symbols in the proper order. We show we are adding when we write the symbols with the largest value first.

Using the cards, try writing all the numbers from 1 to 39 in Roman numerals.

Look back over the Roman numerals you have written. How did you write 4 and 9 in Roman numerals?

When Roman numerals were first used, 4 was written IIII and 9 was written VIIII.

But there is a shortcut.

To understand how the shortcut works, imagine that you want to buy something that costs 4¢ and the only coin you have is a nickel. You can pay the nickel and receive a penny in change.

If you want to pay for something that costs 9¢, you can pay a dime and receive a penny in change.

To pay the exact amount, you subtracted. One less than five is four. One less than ten is nine.

In Roman numerals subtraction is also used. 4 is written IV. When they put the smaller-valued symbol I before V, the Romans meant one less than five. VI means one more than five.

9 is written IX. Because the smaller-valued symbol I comes before X, we know it means one less than ten. XI means one more than ten.

IX means 10−1 or 9

XI means 10+1 or 11

Today we use the shortcut. Because we use the shortcut there can never be more than three of the same symbol in a row.

On page 23, using cards, you wrote the Roman numerals from 1 to 39. Look them over. On your own paper, circle the numerals with more than three of the same symbol in a row. Change them by using the shortcut.

14 was written XIIII. It should be changed to XIV. 19 was written XVIIII. It should be changed to XIX.

How would you change 24? 29? 34? 39?

Which of these numerals can be made shorter?

I	II	III	IIII	V
VI	VII	VIII	VIIII	X
XI	XII	XIII	XIIII	XV
XVI	XVII	XVIII	XVIIII	XX
XXI	XXII	XXIII	XXIIII	XXV
XXVI	XXVII	XXVIII	XXVIIII	XXX
XXXI	XXXII	XXXIII	XXXIIII	XXXV
XXXVI	XXXVII	XXXVIII	XXXVIIII	

There are other symbols in Roman numerals.

L means 50.

C means 100.

D means 500.

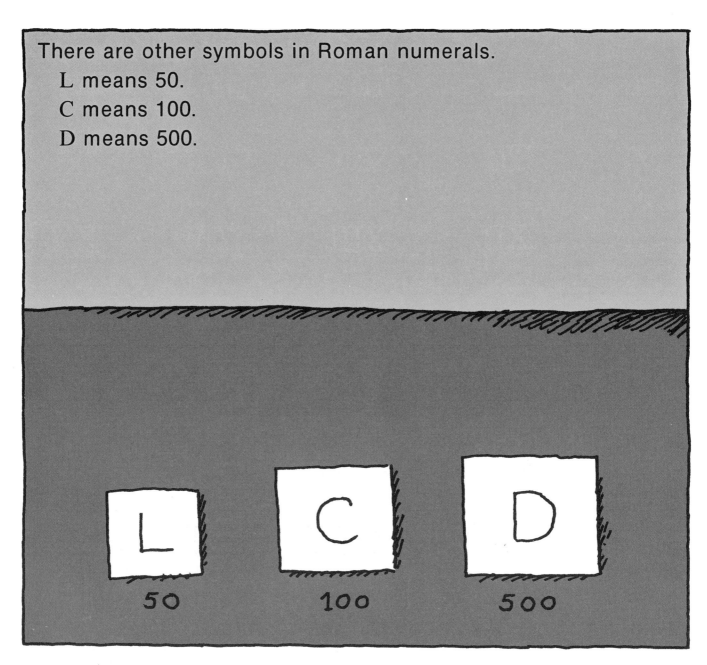

50   100   500

M means 1,000.
$\overline{V}$ means 5,000. (The bar on top means thousands.)
$\overline{X}$ means 10,000. (The bar on top means thousands.)

When you write larger numbers such as 49, first you write the symbols for 40, XL, then you write the symbols for 9, IX. In Roman numerals XLIX means 49.

To write 95, first you write the symbols for 90, XC, then you write the symbol for 5, V. In Roman numerals XCV means 95.

How would you write 67, 75, 88, 89, and 155 in Roman numerals?

Look at clocks, on the sides of buildings and in books. Do you see Roman numerals on some of them? Do you know what they mean?

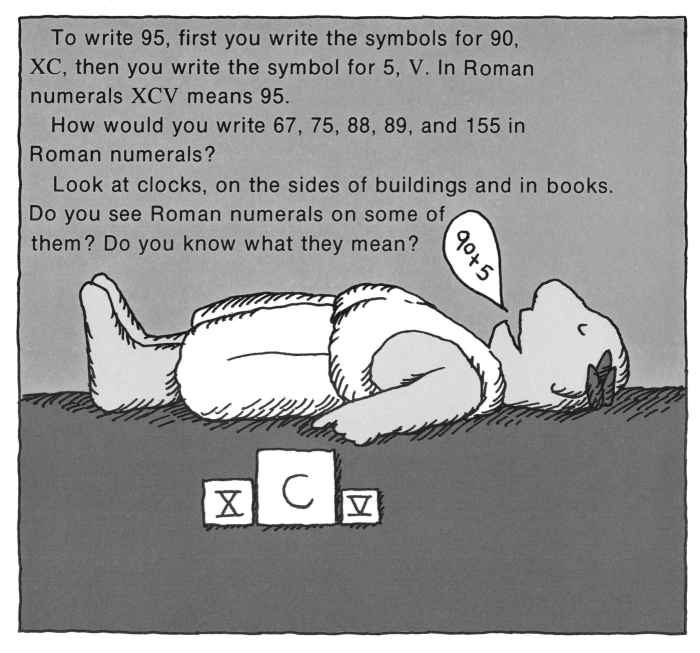

ABOUT THE AUTHOR

David A. Adler has been interested in mathematics since his early years in elementary school. He holds degrees from Queens College and New York University, and is presently a teacher of mathematics in the New York City school system.

In addition to writing several books of fiction for children, Mr. Adler has written two other books in the Young Math Series. They are *Base Five* and *3D, 2D, 1D,* a book about volume, area, and perimeter, which has been selected by the National Science Teachers Association and the Children's Book Council as an Outstanding Science Book for Children.

Along with his wife, Renée, a psychologist, Mr. Adler lives in Briarwood, New York.

ABOUT THE ILLUSTRATOR

Byron Barton has written and illustrated many books for children, including *Hester* and *Buzz, Buzz, Buzz.* He has illustrated other books in the Young Math Series, including *How Little and How Much: A Book About Scales.*

Mr. Barton was born in Pawtucket, Rhode Island. He has lived in Los Angeles and now makes his home in Greenwich Village in New York City.